STEGOSAURUS

by Janet Riehecky
illustrated by Diana Magnuson

THE CHILD'S WORLD

MANKATO, MN

Grateful appreciation is expressed to Bret S. Beall,
Curatorial Coordinator for the Department of Geology,
Field Museum of Natural History, Chicago, Illinois,
who reviewed this book to insure its accuracy.

Library of Congress Cataloging in Publication Data

Riehecky, Janet, 1953-
  Stegosaurus / by Janet Riehecky ; illustrated by Diana L.
Magnuson.
    p. cm. — (Dinosaurs)
    Summary: Describes the probable appearance and behavior of the
stegosaurus, including hypotheses about the arrangement and purpose
of the plates on its back.
    ISBN 0-89565-385-0
    1. Stegosaurus—Juvenile literature.   [1. Stegosaurus.
2. Dinosaurs.]   I. Magnuson, Diana, ill.   II. Title.   III. Series:
Riehecky, Janet, 1953-   Dinosaurs.
QE862.065R54 1988
567.9'7—dc19   88-15347
                                                              CIP
                                                              AC

STEGOSAURUS

Many strange creatures have lived on
the earth. Among the strangest of all
were the dinosaurs.

These reptiles ruled the earth for millions of years, long before any people lived.

These strange creatures had many
strange features. One had very long
claws . . .

and one had very big teeth.

One dinosaur had a huge spiked frill.

Still others had webbed fingers, ridges
on their heads, and mouths like duck bills.

One of the strangest of the dinosaurs was the Stegosaurus (STEG-uh-sawr-us). Its name means "roof lizard" or "covered lizard." It was named that because of the rows of triangular plates on its neck, back, and tail. It had eighteen or twenty plates arranged in two rows.

But these plates were not the only unusual thing about the Stegosaurus.

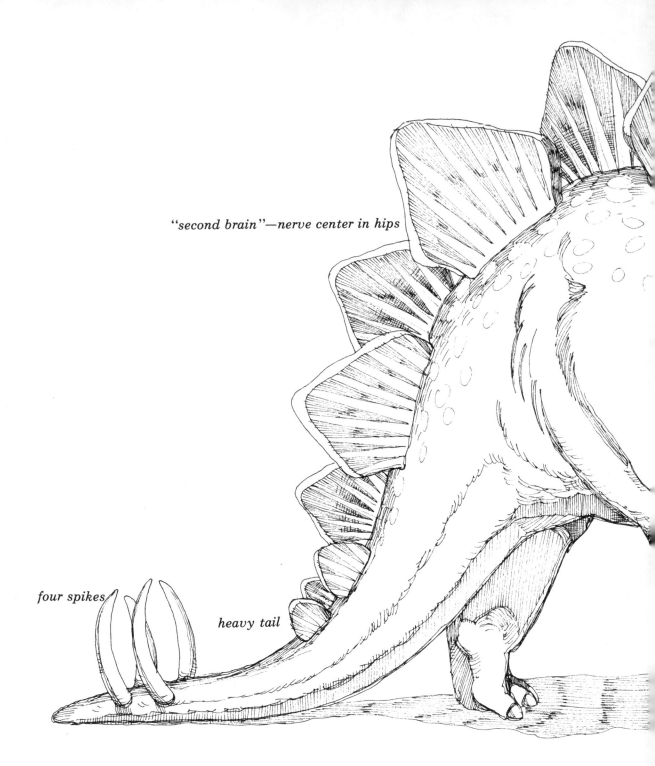

"second brain"—nerve center in hips

four spikes

heavy tail

Imagine what you would look like if you walked on your feet and your elbows! Well, that's what the Stegosaurus looked like.

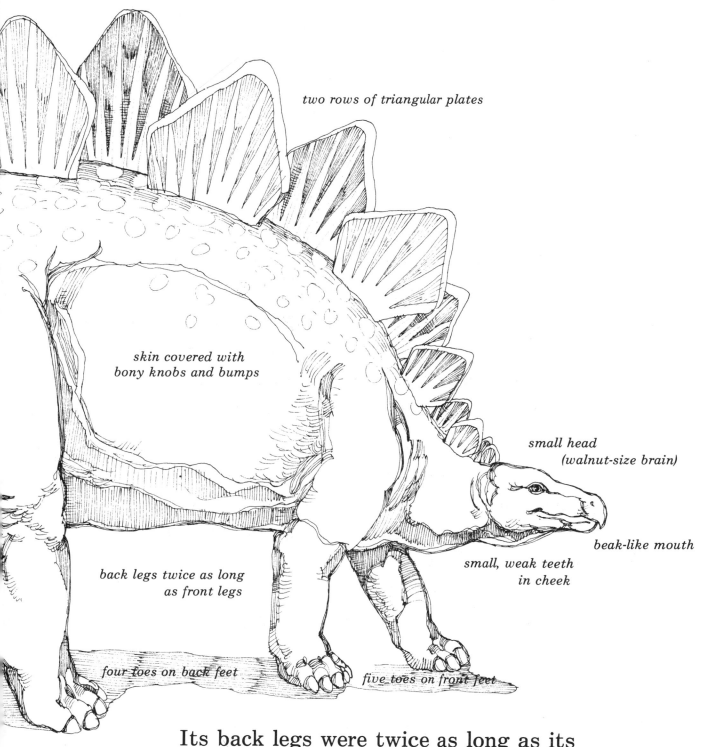

two rows of triangular plates

skin covered with
bony knobs and bumps

small head
(walnut-size brain)

beak-like mouth

small, weak teeth
in cheek

back legs twice as long
as front legs

four toes on back feet

five toes on front feet

Its back legs were twice as long as its
front legs. That meant its hips were stuck
way up in the air (11 feet!), its head and
shoulders were close to the ground, and
its back curved like a slide.

That was certainly a strange shape, but the Stegosaurus had an even stranger mouth—half bird and half reptile!

The front of its mouth was a beak, like that of a parrot or turtle. In the back of its mouth, though, it had rows of small, weak teeth.

As you can imagine, this made it very hard for the Stegosaurus to eat. It could break off a mouthful of plants, but it couldn't really chew them up before swallowing them. The plants just sat in the Stegosaurus' stomach, taking days to digest.

This strange creature not only had trouble eating—it also had trouble thinking.

The Stegosaurus had probably the smallest brain of any dinosaur—it was only as big as a golf ball. That meant the Stegosaurus thought very slowly. And it meant the Stegosaurus needed help from a "second brain" just to move its big body. The "second brain" was in its hips!

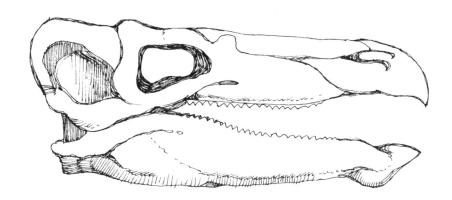

This wasn't really a brain. It was a "nerve center" which helped control the movement of the Stegosaurus legs and tail. Without it, the Stegosaurus might not have been able to move if somebody tried to take a bite out of its back legs. And there were plenty of creatures around who wanted to take a bite out of the Stegosaurus!

The Stegosaurus lived at the same time as the fierce Allosaurus and many other meat eaters. It couldn't run fast, and it couldn't think fast. It had to have some way to protect itself—so it grew a very strange weapon.

Most dinosaurs that needed to defend themselves grew sharp claws on their feet or horns on their heads. But the Stegosaurus did things backwards. It grew four, foot-long spikes on its tail!

These spikes were good weapons and
helped the Stegosaurus, but they were
not good enough to fight off a determined
attack. So the Stegosaurus' best chance
for survival was either to hide from meat
eaters or to stay with a herd of Stegosaurs.

Like any bully, an Allosaurus would rather attack a Stegosaurus found alone than one with a lot of friends nearby.

There have been lots of arguments about the Stegosaurus, especially about the plates on its back. Scientists have wondered whether there was one row of plates or two, whether they stood up straight or lay down flat, and whether they were arranged in pairs or alternated. They have also wondered what the plates were for.

They weren't dinner plates—but they
may have helped keep the Stegosaurus
from becoming someone else's dinner.

Or the plates may have worked to keep
the Stegosaurus from becoming too hot.
Their position and shape seemed designed
to pull heat from the body of the Stegosaurus and let the wind carry it away.

Or the plates may have been just for display, to help the Stegosaurus attract a mate.

Scientists have considered all of these ideas, but they have not been able to agree. They continue to study the plates, but they may never know for sure why the Stegosaurus had them.

Scientists also don't know much about the kind of life the Stegosaurus led. They think Stegosaurs traveled in herds, living near swamps and rivers and eating plants that grew close to the ground.

Scientists think the Stegosaurus laid
eggs and that it probably left its babies
on their own to take care of themselves.
But they don't know this for sure.

There will always be things we don't
know about the Stegosaurus.

But that's part of the fascination of this strange creature.

 **Dinosaur Fun**

There are several museums throughout the United States that have Stegosaurus skeletons, casts, or fossils on display. If you live near one of these museums or will be traveling near one, you may want to stop in and say hello to Stegosaurus! These museums all have many other dinosaurs on display too:

American Museum of Natural
   History
Central Park West/79th St.
New York, New York 10024

Denver Museum of Natural
   History
City Park
Denver, Colorado 80205

University of Michigan Exhibit
Alexander G. Ruthven
   Museum
1109 Geddes Avenue
Ann Arbor, Michigan 48109

National Museum of Natural
   History
Smithsonian Institution
Washington, D.C. 20560

Carnegie Museum of Natural
   History
4400 Forbes Avenue
Pittsburgh, Pennsylvania 15213

Dinosaur Valley
Museum of Western Colorado
4th and Main
Grand Junction, Colorado 81501